Chicken Salad

Recipes

Laura Sommers is **The Recipe Lady!**

She is the #1 Best Selling Author of over 80 recipe books.

She is a loving wife and mother who lives on a small farm in Baltimore County, Maryland and has a passion for all things domestic especially when it comes to saving money. She has a profitable eBay business and is a couponing addict. Follow her tips and tricks to learn how to make delicious meals on a budget, save money or to learn the latest life hack!

Visit her Amazon Author Page to see her latest books:

amazon.com/author/laurasommers

Visit the Recipe Lady's blog for even more great recipes and to learn which books are **FREE** for download each week:

http://the-recipe-lady.blogspot.com/

Subscribe to The Recipe Lady blog through Amazon and have recipes and updates sent directly to your Kindle:

The Recipe Lady Blog through Amazon

Laura Sommers is also an Extreme Couponer and Penny Hauler! If you would like to find out how to get things for **FREE** with coupons or how to get things for only a **PENNY**, then visit her couponing blog **Penny Items and Freebies**

http://penny-items-and-freebies.blogspot.com/

Introduction

Have you ever thought about all the different ways to make chicken salad? If you have never thought beyond the traditional chicken and mayonnaise combination, then buckle up because you are in for a wild ride. There are many ways to make chicken salad and this cookbook is full of delicious mouth-watering recipes for you to try. There are so many chicken salad recipes that you will always have something new to enjoy and to make to impress your friends. And chicken salad is low carb which means it is great for those on a low carb diet. Substitute the low fat version of mayonnaise, sour cream or dressing and the recipe becomes low calorie as well.

Chicken salad can be served on bread, in a pita, in a wrap on a bed of lettuce or plain. You will find so many different ways to enjoy chicken salad in this cookbook that you will never get bored.

Chutney Chicken Salad

Ingredients:

1/2 cup mayonnaise
1/2 cup chutney
1 tsp. curry powder
2 tsps. lime zest
1/4 cup fresh lime juice
1/2 tsp. salt
4 cups diced, cooked chicken breast meat

Directions:

1. In a large bowl, whisk together the mayonnaise, chutney, curry powder, lime zest, lime juice and salt.
2. Add chicken and toss with the dressing until well coated.
3. Add more mayonnaise to taste, if desired.
4. Cover and refrigerate until serving.

Dill Pickle Chicken Salad

Ingredients:

1 cooked, boneless chicken breast half, chopped
2 stalks celery, chopped
3 tbsps. mayonnaise
1/2 onion, finely diced
2 dill pickles, chopped
1/4 tsp. garlic powder
Salt and pepper to taste

Directions:

1. Combine the chicken, celery, mayonnaise, onion and pickle.
2. Mix well.
3. Season with the garlic powder, salt and pepper.
4. Serve with lettuce on fresh crusty bread or bun.

Feta Chicken Salad

Ingredients:

3 cups diced cooked chicken
2 large stalks celery, diced
1 red bell pepper, seeded and diced
1/2 red onion, diced
6 tbsps. mayonnaise
6 tbsps. sour cream
1 (4 oz.) package feta cheese, crumbled
2 tsps. dried dill weed
1 pinch salt and pepper to taste

Directions:

1. In a serving bowl, mix together the chicken, celery, and red onion.
2. In a separate bowl, stir together the mayonnaise, sour cream, feta cheese, and dill.
3. Pour over the chicken mixture, and stir to blend.
4. Taste, and season with salt and pepper as needed.

Ginger Chicken Salad

Ingredients:

2 cups cubed cooked chicken breast
3/4 cup seedless green grapes, halved
1/2 cup chopped celery
1/2 cup chopped pecans
1/4 cup minced fresh parsley
1/2 cup mayonnaise
1/4 cup sour cream
3/4 tsp. freshly grated ginger
1/8 tsp. ground white pepper

Directions:

1. Combine chicken, grapes, celery, pecans, and parsley in a bowl.
2. Whisk mayonnaise, sour cream, ginger, and white pepper together in a separate bowl; gently stir into chicken mixture.
3. Cover bowl with plastic wrap and refrigerate until chilled, 1 to 2 hours.

Curry Chicken Salad with Grapes

Ingredients:

1/2 cup butter
2 cups mayonnaise
1/4 cup minced garlic
2 tbsps. chopped fresh parsley
1 tsp. curry powder
4 cups shredded cooked chicken
2 cups halved red grapes
1/2 cup toasted slivered almonds

Directions:

1. Heat butter in a large saucepan over low heat until melted.
2. Remove from heat and cool to room temperature.
3. Stir mayonnaise, garlic, parsley, and curry powder into butter until evenly incorporated.
4. Fold in chicken, grapes, and almonds.
5. Transfer mixture to a serving bowl and cover with plastic wrap. Refrigerate until flavors have blended, at least 1 hour.

Chicken Curry Salad

Ingredients:

5 skinless, boneless chicken breast halves
1 cup mayonnaise
3/4 cup chutney
1 tsp. curry powder
1/4 tsp. pepper
2/3 cup chopped pecans
1 cup seedless grapes, halved
1/2 cup chopped onion

Directions:

1. In a large saucepan, simmer chicken breasts in water for about 7 to 10 minutes, or until cooked through.
2. Drain, cool, and tear into small pieces with a fork.
3. In a large bowl, combine mayonnaise, chutney, curry powder, and pepper. Stir in chicken, pecans, grapes, and onions.
4. Chill.

Chicken Salad with Grapes and Apples

Ingredients:

2 tbsps. mayonnaise
1 cup cubed cooked chicken
1 cup halved grapes
1 Gala apple, diced
1/3 cup diced red onion
1 tbsp. honey mustard
1/4 tsp. garlic powder
1/8 tsp. ground black pepper

Directions:

1. Mix mayonnaise, chicken, grapes, apple, onion, honey mustard, garlic powder, and black pepper in a bowl.
2. Serve and enjoy!

Curry Chicken Salad

Ingredients:

3 cooked skinless, boneless chicken breast halves, chopped
3 stalks celery, chopped
1/2 cup mayonnaise
2 tsps. curry powder

Directions:

1. In a medium bowl, stir together the chicken, celery, mayonnaise, and curry powder.
2. Serve and enjoy!

Cranberry Chicken Salad

Ingredients:

2 cooked chicken breast halves, chopped
1/2 cup mayonnaise, or to taste
2 green onions, chopped
1/2 cup sweetened dried cranberries
1/4 green apple, shredded
1/4 cup chopped pecans
1 tbsp. lime juice
1 pinch salt and black pepper to taste
1/4 tsp. dried dill weed

Directions:

1. Mix together the chicken and mayonnaise in a bowl, stir to coat well, then stir in the green onions, dried cranberries, apple, pecans, lime juice, salt, pepper, and dill weed. Serve immediately, or refrigerate several hours or overnight (the flavor just gets better).

Fruity Chicken Salad

Ingredients:

1 apple, cored and diced
1/2 cup seedless red grapes, halved
1/2 cup chopped toasted pecans
1/2 tsp. apple pie spice, or to taste
3/4 cup mayonnaise
4 skinless, boneless chicken breast halves - cooked and diced

Directions:

1. In a bowl, lightly mix the apple, grapes, pecans, apple pie spice, and mayonnaise together until thoroughly combined; stir in the chicken breast meat. Chill until cold.

Holiday Chicken Salad

Ingredients:

4 cups cubed, cooked chicken meat
1 cup mayonnaise
1 tsp. paprika
1 1/2 cups dried cranberries
1 cup chopped celery
2 green onions, chopped
1/2 cup minced green bell pepper
1 cup chopped pecans
1 tsp. seasoning salt ground black pepper to taste

Directions:

1. In a medium bowl, mix together mayonnaise with paprika and seasoned salt. Blend in dried cranberries, celcry, bell pepper, onion, and nuts. Add chopped chicken, and mix well. Season with black pepper to taste. Chill 1 hour.

Tarragon Chicken Salad

Ingredients:

3 cups cubed, cooked chicken meat
1 1/2 cups chopped celery
1/4 cup chopped fresh chives
1/2 cup plain yogurt
1/4 cup reduced fat sour cream
1 1/2 tsps. dried tarragon
2 tbsps. blanched slivered almonds salt and pepper to taste

Directions:

1. In a large bowl, combine chicken, celery, chives or green onions, yogurt, sour cream or mayonnaise, and tarragon; mix lightly. Cover, and refrigerate for 1 hour.
2. Place nuts in a dry skillet. Toast over medium heat, turning frequently, until nuts are fragrant and lightly browned. Add almonds to chicken salad, and season with salt and pepper to taste. Serve immediately.

Greek Chicken Salad

Ingredients:

2 cups cubed, cooked chicken meat
1/2 cup sliced carrots
1/2 cup sliced cucumber
1/4 cup sliced black olives
1/4 cup crumbled feta cheese
1/4 cup Italian-style salad dressing

Directions:

1. In a large bowl combine the chicken, carrots, cucumber, olives and cheese. Gently mix together. Add the salad dressing and mix well.
2. Cover and refrigerate. Let flavors marinate for at least 1 hour. Serve on a bed of lettuce if desired.

Mediterranean Chicken Salad

Ingredients:

1 1/2 cups sun-dried tomato and oregano salad dressing
4 skinless, boneless chicken breast halves
2 red bell peppers, halved and seeded
1 head romaine lettuce, torn into bite-size pieces
1 cup black olives, drained
4 oz. feta cheese, crumbled
1/2 cup sun-dried tomato and oregano salad dressing

Directions:

1. In a shallow dish, arrange chicken breasts and evenly cover with 1 cup of the salad dressing.
2. Cover tightly and marinate in the refrigerator for 20 minutes to an hour.
3. Preheat your grill to high heat. While grill is preheating, arrange lettuce, olives and feta cheese in a salad bowl.
4. Remove chicken from marinade and place on grill.
5. Cook chicken breasts for 6 to 8 minutes per side.
6. Arrange peppers on grill, and baste with the reserved 1/2 cup dressing.
7. The peppers will need only a few minutes, be careful not to burn them!
8. Remove chicken and peppers from the grill and, when cool enough to handle, slice into strips.
9. Arrange peppers and chicken on top of the salad and serve with the last 1/2 cup of dressing.

Chinese Chicken Salad

Ingredients:

3 tbsps. hoisin sauce
2 tbsps. peanut butter
2 tsps. brown sugar
3/4 tsp. hot chile paste
1 tsp. grated fresh ginger
3 tbsps. rice wine vinegar
1 tbsp. sesame oil
1 pound skinless, boneless chicken breast halves
16 (3.5 inch square) wonton wrappers, shredded
4 cups romaine lettuce, torn
2 cups shredded carrots
1 bunch green onions, chopped
1/4 cup chopped fresh cilantro

Directions:

1. To prepare the dressing, whisk together the hoisin sauce, peanut butter, brown sugar, chili paste, ginger, vinegar, and sesame oil.
2. Grill or broil the chicken breasts until cooked, about 10 minutes.
3. An instant-read thermometer inserted into the center should read 165 degrees F (74 degrees C).
4. Cool and slice.
5. Preheat oven to 350 degrees F (175 C).
6. Spray a large shallow pan with nonstick vegetable spray; arrange shredded wontons in a single layer and bake until golden brown, about 20 minutes. Cool.
7. In a large bowl, combine the chicken, wontons, lettuce, carrots, green onions and cilantro.
8. Toss with dressing and serve.

Chicken Fiesta Salad

Ingredients:

2 skinless, boneless chicken breast halves
1 (1.27 oz.) packet dry fajita seasoning, divided
1 tbsp. vegetable oil
1 (15 oz.) can black beans, rinsed and drained
1 (11 oz.) can Mexican-style corn
1/2 cup salsa
1 (10 oz.) package mixed salad greens
1 onion, chopped 1 tomato, cut into wedges

Directions:

1. Rub chicken evenly with 1/2 the fajita seasoning.
2. Heat the oil in a skillet over medium heat, and cook the chicken 8 minutes on each side, or until juices run clear; set aside.
3. In a large saucepan, mix beans, corn, salsa and other 1/2 of fajita seasoning. Heat over medium heat until warm.
4. Prepare the salad by tossing the greens, onion and tomato.
5. Top salad with chicken and dress with the bean and corn mixture.

Easy Chinese Chicken Salad

Ingredients:

1 rotisserie chicken, meat removed and shredded
1/2 medium head cabbage, chopped
4 green onions, sliced
1 (3 oz.) package ramen noodles
3 tbsps. sesame seeds
3 tbsps. slivered almonds

Dressing Ingredients:

1/2 cup olive oil
3 tbsps. apple cider vinegar
2 tbsps. white sugar
1 tsp. salt
1 tsp. ground black pepper

Directions:

1. Toss chicken meat, cabbage, onions, ramen noodles, sesame seeds, and almonds together in a large bowl.
2. Beat olive oil, vinegar, sugar, salt, and pepper together in a small bowl.
3. Drizzle over the salad and toss to coat.

Chicken Salad With Pine Nuts and Raisins

Ingredients:

1 1/2 cups cubed French bread
1/2 cup sour cream
1/3 cup mayonnaise
2 tbsps. lemon juice
2 tsps. Dijon mustard
2 tsps. honey
1 tbsp. chopped fresh rosemary
1/8 tsp. salt
1/4 tsp. ground black pepper
1 pound skinless, boneless chicken breasts
2 stalks celery, chopped
1/3 cup golden raisins
1 tbsp. lemon zest 6 leaves romaine lettuce
6 leaves Radicchio, raw
2 tsps. lemon juice
1 tsp. olive oil
3 slices red onion
1/3 cup pine nuts, toasted

Directions:

1. Preheat oven to 350 degrees F (175 degrees C).
2. Spray a baking sheet with olive oil or non-stick cooking spray.
3. Prepare the croutons by spreading bread cubes over prepared baking sheet.
4. Lightly spray cubes with oil or cooking spray and bake for 20 minutes or until golden brown.
5. Remove from oven and cool.
6. Prepare the dressing by whisking together the sour cream, mayonnaise, lemon juice, mustard, honey, rosemary, salt and pepper.
7. Cover and refrigerate until ready to serve.
8. Prepare the salad by placing the chicken in a pan and cover with water. Bring just to a boil, cover and reduce the heat to medium-low.
9. Cook 10 minutes, or until chicken is cooked through.
10. Remove from heat, drain and cool; dice or pull into shreds.
11. Combine the chicken with the celery, raisins and lemon peel.
12. When ready to serve, stir together the lemon juice and olive oil.

13. Tear the lettuce into small pieces and toss with the lemon and oil mixture.
14. Divide between plates and top with the chicken salad.
15. Garnish with onion rings, a sprinkling of pine nuts and the croutons.

Miracle Whip and Olives Chicken Salad

Ingredients:

1 cup canned chicken, chopped
1 cup celery, chopped
1/4 cup onion, chopped
1/4 cup olives, chopped
1 hard boiled egg
1/2 cup Miracle Whip
Poultry seasoning to taste
Iceberg lettuce

Directions:

1. Chop finely the chicken, onion, boiled egg (boil it for about 12 minutes for perfect texture) and celery. Shred or chop the lettuce.
2. Mix everything together thoroughly, including the chopped olives, and put half on each of two bread slices.
3. Top the spread on the sandwich with chopped iceberg lettuce, then cover each with the remaining bread slices.

Creamy Pesto Chicken Salad

Ingredients:

1 lb. boneless, skinless chicken breast, trimmed
1/4 cup pesto¼ cup mayonnaise
3 tbsps. finely chopped red onion
2 tbsps. extra-virgin olive oil
2 tbsps. red-wine vinegar
1/4 tsp. salt
1/4 tsp. ground pepper
1 5-oz. package mixed salad greens (about 8 cups)

Directions:

1. Place chicken in a medium saucepan and add water to cover by 1 inch. Bring to a boil.
2. Cover, reduce heat to low and simmer gently until no longer pink in the middle, 10 to 15 minutes.
3. Transfer to a clean cutting board; shred into bite-size pieces when cool enough to handle.
4. Combine pesto, mayonnaise and onion in a medium bowl.
5. Add the chicken and toss to coat.
6. Whisk oil, vinegar, salt and pepper in a large bowl.
7. Add greens and tomatoes and toss to coat.
8. Divide the green salad among 4 plates and top with the chicken salad.

Nutty Pesto Chicken Salad

Ingredients:

1/2 cup mayonnaise
1/3 cup plain yogurt
1/3 cup pesto
1 1/2 tbsps. fresh lemon juice
1/2 tsp. salt
1/2 tsp. black pepper
4 cups cubed chicken breast
1 cup diced celery
1/3 cup chopped walnuts, toasted
1 (12-oz.) bottle roasted red bell peppers, drained and chopped

Directions:

1. Combine first 6 ingredients in a large bowl, stirring with a whisk.
2. Stir in chicken, celery, and walnuts.
3. Spread 1/2 cup of salad onto each of 10 bread slices.
4. Top each serving with about 2 tbsps. bell pepper, 1 lettuce leaf, and one bread slice.

Pesto Chicken Salad

Ingredients:

1/2 cup mayonnaise
1/2 cup store-bought pesto
Kosher salt
Black pepper
1 2 pound chicken, meat chopped

Directions:

1. In a large bowl, combine the mayonnaise, pesto, ½ tsp. salt, and ¼ tsp. pepper.
2. Toss with the chicken.

Chicken Salad With Pine Nuts and Raisins

Ingredients:

1 1/2 cups cubed French bread
1/2 cup sour cream
1/3 cup mayonnaise
2 tbsps. lemon juice
2 tsps. Dijon-style prepared mustard
2 tsps. honey
1 tbsp. chopped fresh rosemary
1/8 tsp. salt
1/4 tsp. ground black pepper
1 pound skinless, boneless chicken breasts
2 stalks celery, chopped
1/3 cup golden raisins
1 tbsp. lemon zest
6 leaves romaine lettuce
6 leaves Radicchio, raw
2 tsps. lemon juice
1 tsp. olive oil
3 slices red onion
1/3 cup pine nuts, toasted

Directions:

1. Preheat oven to 350 degrees F (175 degrees C).
2. Spray a baking sheet with olive oil or non-stick cooking spray.
3. Prepare the croutons by spreading bread cubes over prepared baking sheet.
4. Lightly spray cubes with oil or cooking spray and bake for 20 minutes or until golden brown.
5. Remove from oven and cool.
6. Prepare the dressing by whisking together the sour cream, mayonnaise, lemon juice, mustard, honey, rosemary, salt and pepper.
7. Cover and refrigerate until ready to serve.
8. Prepare the salad by placing the chicken in a pan and cover with water. Bring just to a boil, cover and reduce the heat to medium-low.
9. Cook 10 minutes, or until chicken is cooked through.
10. Remove from heat, drain and cool; dice or pull into shreds.
11. Combine the chicken with the celery, raisins and lemon peel.

12. When ready to serve, stir together the lemon juice and olive oil.
13. Tear the lettuce into small pieces and toss with the lemon and oil mixture.
14. Divide between plates and top with the chicken salad.
15. Garnish with onion rings, a sprinkling of pine nuts and the croutons.

Southern Chicken Salad

Ingredients:

1/2 cup mayonnaise
3 tbsps. buttermilk
1/4 cup minced green onions
2 tbsps. chopped fresh dill
1/4 tsp. freshly ground black pepper
1 pound skinless, boneless chicken breasts
1 cup dry white wine
1 sprig fresh dill weed
1/8 tsp. freshly ground black pepper
1 1/2 cups seedless grapes
1 cup thinly sliced celery
8 leaves red leaf lettuce - rinsed
1/2 cup chopped salted cashews
5 sprigs fresh dill weed, for garnish

Dressing Directions:

1. Whisk the mayonnaise, green onions, buttermilk, dill and ground black pepper in a small bowl to blend.
2. Cover and chill.

Salad Directions:

1. Arrange the chicken in a heavy, medium size skillet. Add the wine, dill and ground black pepper.
2. Season with salt. If necessary, add water to cover the chicken.
3. Simmer over medium low heat until chicken is just cooked through, turning once (about 11 minutes).
4. Transfer chicken to a plate and let cool.
5. Cut chicken into 1/2 inch pieces.
6. Place in a large bowl.
7. Add the grapes and the celery and mix in the dressing to thoroughly coat the mixture.
8. Season with salt and pepper to taste.
9. Cover and refrigerate for at least 20 minutes to develop the flavors.
10. Arrange the lettuce leaves on plates, mound on the salad and sprinkle with nuts.
11. Garnish with fresh dill and serve.

Curried Hawaiian Chicken Salad

Ingredients:

6 boneless, skinless chicken breasts, cubed
3 cups mayonnaise
1 tbsp. curry powder
1 tsp. lemon juice
1 tbsp. soy sauce
2 1/2 cups slivered almonds, toasted
1 pound seedless green grapes, halved
2 cups chopped celery
1 (8 oz.) can sliced water chestnuts
1 (20 oz.) can pineapple chunks, drained
Paprika, for garnish

Directions:

1. Place chicken in a large pot of lightly salted water, and bring to a boil; simmer until tender and cooked through, about 25 minutes.
2. Drain, set aside. When cool enough to handle, chop coarsely, and place into a large bowl.
3. In a separate bowl, stir together mayonnaise, curry powder, lemon juice, and soy sauce.
4. Stir into the chopped chicken 2 1/4 cups of the toasted almonds. Stir in grapes, celery, water chestnuts, and pineapple.
5. Gently fold in all but 1/2 cup of the dressing.
6. Cover, and refrigerate salad and reserved dressing for several hours (or overnight).
7. Before serving, adjust dressing to taste, and garnish with paprika and remaining 1/4 cup almonds.

Lemon Chicken Salad

Ingredients:

1/2 cup White Cooking Wine
1 lb. boneless chicken breasts, skinned
1 cup pea pods, blanched
3/4 cup sliced celery
1/4 cup sliced green onions
1/2 cup mayonnaise
1 tsp. grated lemon peel
Pepper to taste
1/2 cup toasted slivered almonds
Lettuce

Directions:

1. Place cooking wine and chicken in large saucepan.
2. Add enough water to cover. Bring to a boil; reduce heat.
3. Simmer 10 minutes or until chicken is tender and no longer pink.
4. Let chicken cool in liquid 45 minutes.
5. Drain; cut chicken into bite-sized pieces.
6. In large bowl, combine chicken, pea pods, celery, onions, mayonnaise, lemon peel and pepper; mix well.
7. Cover; refrigerate 1 to 2 hours to blend flavors.
8. Just before serving, stir in almonds.
9. To serve, spoon chicken salad onto lettuce-lined plates.

Chipotle Chicken Salad

Ingredients:

1 1/2 pounds boneless, skinless chicken breast halves
1 red onion, cut into wedges
1 tbsp. olive oil
Salt and pepper
1 cup chopped jarred roasted red peppers
3 tbsps. sour cream
2 tbsps. mayonnaise
1 tbsp. minced seeded chipotle chiles in adobo
2 tsps. adobo sauce
1 tbsp. lime juice
1/3 cup finely chopped fresh cilantro

Directions:

1. Preheat oven to 350 degrees F. Place chicken on a rimmed, foil-lined baking sheet and surround with red onion wedges.
2. Drizzle with olive oil and sprinkle lightly with salt and pepper.
3. Bake 20 minutes, until onions are softened and chicken is cooked through (cut to test).
4. Let cool 10 minutes on baking sheet, then transfer chicken to cutting board and cut into half-inch cubes.
5. Coarsely chop onion.
6. Transfer chicken and onion to a large bowl and let cool to room temperature.
7. Stir in roasted peppers.
8. In a small bowl, combine sour cream, mayonnaise, chipotles, adobo sauce and lime juice; stir to combine.
9. Pour dressing over chicken mixture and toss to coat evenly.
10. Sprinkle salad with cilantro and serve.

Buffalo Chicken Salad

Ingredients:

1 pound cubed chicken
1 cup celery, finely chopped
3/4 cup mayonnaise
3 tbsps. buffalo sauce

Directions:

1. Cube the chicken and put in a bowl.
2. Toss with the remaining ingredients.
3. Serve and enjoy!

Hazelnut Apple Chicken Salad

Ingredients:

1/4 cup mayonnaise
1 1/2 tbsps. chopped fresh tarragon
2 tsps. water 1/8 tsp. freshly ground black pepper
2 cups chopped chicken breast
1/2 cup chopped Granny Smith apple
3 tbsps. chopped toasted hazelnuts

Directions:

1. Stir together mayonnaise, tarragon, 2 tsps. water, and black pepper in a large bowl.
2. Add the chicken, apple, and hazelnuts to dressing; toss gently to combine.
3. Cover and chill until ready to serve.

Chicken Caesar Salad

Ingredients:

1 pound boneless cooked chicken, cubed
1 cup celery, finely chopped
3/4 cup creamy Caesar dressing
3-5 large Romaine lettuce leaves, chopped

Directions:

1. Cube the chicken and put in a bowl.
2. Toss with the remaining ingredients.
3. Serve on a sandwich and enjoy!

Whiskey and Beer BBQ Chicken Salad

Ingredients:

4 cups boneless cooked chicken, cubed
1 cup barbecue sauce
1 1/2 cups lager beer, such as a pilsner
2 tbsps. whiskey
1 tsp. seasoned salt
1 tsp. garlic-pepper blend
1/2 tsp. ground mustard
2 tsps. Buffalo Wings Sauce

Directions:

1. In 2-quart saucepan, heat sauce ingredients to boiling over medium heat, stirring frequently.
2. Reduce heat to medium-low and simmer 20 minutes, stirring occasionally to prevent scorching.
3. In medium microwavable bowl, place chicken; cover.
4. Microwave on high 4 to 5 minutes or until hot.
5. Add shredded chicken to sauce in saucepan, stir to coat.
6. Place about 1/3 cup chicken mixture on bottom of each slider bun.
7. Top with bun top.
8. Garnish each sandwich with green olive.

Cantaloupe and Chicken Salad

Ingredients:

1/4 cup plain yogurt
1/4 cup mayonnaise or salad dressing
1 tbsp. fresh lemon juice
1 tbsp. chopped fresh chives
1/4 tsp. salt
5 cups
1 1/2-inch pieces cantaloupe
2 1/2 cups cut-up cooked chicken
1 cup red or green grapes, cut in half
1 medium cucumber, cut into strips

Directions:

1. Mix yogurt and mayonnaise in large bowl.
2. Stir in lemon juice, chives and salt.
3. 2 Stir in remaining ingredients.
4. Serve immediately, or refrigerate until chilled, at least 2 hours but no longer than 24 hours.

Lemon Mint Chicken Salad

Ingredients:

1 pkg. (16 oz.) uncooked bow-tie (farfalle) pasta
7 cups cubed cooked chicken
5 cups cubed cantaloupe
3 cups thinly sliced celery
2 cups dried cherries
1 cup sliced green onions

Dressing Ingredients:

2 (8 oz. each) containers lemon yogurt
1/2 cup reduced-calorie mayonnaise or salad dressing
1 to 2 tbsps. chopped fresh mint
1 tbsp. grated lemon peel
1 1/2 tsps. salt
1/2 tsp. pepper

Garnish Ingredients:

1/4 cup sliced almonds, toasted

Directions:

1. Cook pasta as directed on package to desired doneness.
2. Drain; rinse with cold water.
3. In a large bowl, mix pasta and remaining salad ingredients.
4. In medium bowl, mix dressing ingredients.
5. Add dressing to salad; mix well.
6. Cover.
7. Refrigerate 3 hours to blend flavors.
8. Just before serving, sprinkle with almonds.

Avocado Chicken Salad

Ingredients:

2 tbsps. olive oil
2 tbsps. fresh lime juice
3/8 tsp. kosher salt
1/8 tsp. freshly ground black pepper
2 cups shredded chicken
1/4 cup chopped fresh cilantro
3/4 cup refrigerated fresh salsa
1 ripe avocado, peeled and chopped
3 oz. tortilla chips

Directions:

1. Combine first 4 ingredients in a medium bowl, stirring with a whisk.
2. Add chicken and cilantro; toss to combine.
3. Gently fold in salsa and avocado.
4. Serve with chips.

Honey-Chicken Salad

Ingredients:

4 cups chopped cooked chicken
3 celery ribs, diced (about 1 1/2 cups)
1 cup sweetened dried cranberries
1/2 cup chopped pecans, toasted
1 1/2 cups mayonnaise
1/3 cup honey
1/4 tsp. salt
1/4 tsp. pepper
Chopped toasted pecans for garnish

Directions:

Combine first 4 ingredients.
1. Whisk together mayonnaise and next 3 ingredients.
2. Add to chicken mixture, stirring gently until combined.
3. Garnish, if desired.

Rosemary Chicken Salad

Ingredients:

3 cups chopped roasted skinless, boneless chicken breasts (about 3/4 pound)
1/3 cup chopped green onions
1/4 cup chopped smoked almonds
1/4 cup plain fat-free yogurt
1/4 cup light mayonnaise
1 tsp. chopped fresh rosemary
1 tsp. Dijon mustard
1/8 tsp. salt
1/8 tsp. freshly ground black pepper
10 slices whole-grain bread

Directions:

1. Combine first 9 ingredients, stirring well.
2. Spread about 2/3 cup of chicken mixture over each of 5 bread slices, and top with remaining bread slices.
3. Cut sandwiches diagonally in half.

Apricots and Bok Choy Chicken Salad

Ingredients:

1/3 cup canola mayonnaise
1 tsp. grated orange rind
2 tbsps. fresh orange juice
1 1/2 tsps. distilled white vinegar
1 tsp. grated peeled fresh ginger
1/2 tsp. kosher salt
1/4 tsp. sugar
1/8 tsp. black pepper
6 cups sliced baby bok choy
1 cup sliced radishes
1/3 cup chopped dried apricots
1/4 cup toasted slivered almonds
3 oz. chicken breast, chopped

Directions:

1. Combine mayonnaise, orange rind, orange juice, vinegar, ginger, salt, sugar, and black pepper in a large bowl.
2. Add bok choy, radishes, dried apricots, almonds, dark meat chicken, and chicken breast; toss.

Chicken Horseradish Salad

Ingredients:

3 cups chopped cooked chicken (about 4 skinned and boned chicken breast halves)
1/2 cup minced green onions
2 celery ribs, chopped
1/2 cup chopped pecans, toasted
2/3 cup light mayonnaise
2 to 3 tbsps. prepared horseradish
2 tsps. fresh lemon juice
1/2 tsp. grated lemon rind
1/4 tsp. salt
1/2 tsp. pepper

Directions:

1. Stir together all ingredients in a large bowl.
2. Cover and chill at least 2 hours before serving.

Chicken and Edamame Couscous Salad

Ingredients:

3/4 cup water
2/3 cup uncooked whole-wheat couscous
3/4 cup frozen shelled edamame
3 tbsps. fresh orange juice
2 tbsps. extra-virgin olive oil
1 tbsp. cider vinegar
2 tsps. honey
1/2 tsp. salt
1/2 tsp. black pepper
2 cups coarsely chopped baby spinach
2 cups shredded skinless, boneless rotisserie chicken breast
1/3 cup thinly sliced green onions
1/4 cup coarsely chopped dried cranberries
3 tbsps. chopped unsalted, dry-roasted peanuts

Directions:

1. Bring 3/4 cup water to a boil in a saucepan; stir in couscous.
2. Remove from heat; cover and let stand 5 minutes.
3. Fluff couscous with a fork.
4. Transfer to a bowl.
5. Cook edamame according to package directions; drain.
6. Rinse with cold water; drain.
7. While edamame cooks, combine orange juice and next 5 ingredients (through pepper), stirring well with a whisk.
8. Add edamame, spinach, and next 3 ingredients (through cranberries) to couscous.
9. Pour orange juice mixture over salad; toss to coat.
10. Sprinkle with chopped peanuts.

Creamy Blueberry Chicken Salad

Ingredients:

1/2 cup thinly vertically sliced red onion
1/3 cup diced celery
1/4 cup torn fresh basil
3 cups shredded chicken
1/2 tsp. kosher salt, divided
1/2 cup plain Greek yogurt
2 1/2 tbsps. fresh lemon juice, divided
1 tbsp. honey
2 cups fresh blueberries
1 (5-oz.) package baby arugula
2 tsps. extra-virgin olive oil
1/4 tsp. freshly ground black pepper

Directions:

1. Combine first 4 ingredients in a medium bowl; sprinkle with 1/4 tsp. salt.
2. Combine yogurt, 1 tbsp. lemon juice, and honey in a small bowl, stirring with a whisk. Add yogurt mixture to chicken mixture; toss to coat.
3. Gently stir in blueberries.
4. Place arugula, remaining 1 1/2 tbsps. lemon juice, oil, remaining 1/4 tsp. salt, and pepper in a bowl; toss to coat.
5. Divide arugula mixture evenly among 6 plates.
6. Top each serving with about 3/4 cup chicken mixture.

Mango and Apple Chicken Salad

Ingredients:

1/2 cup plain Greek-style yogurt
3 tbsps. olive oil
2 tbsps. lemon juice (from
1/2 large lemon)
1 tbsp. honey
1 1/2 tsps. curry powder
Salt and pepper
3 cups shredded chicken
1 med. Granny Smith apple, cored, diced
1 mango, peeled, pitted, diced
1 rib celery, diced
3 tbsps. finely chopped red onion

Directions:

1. In a small bowl, whisk together yogurt, olive oil, lemon juice, honey, curry powder and 1/2 tsp. salt.
2. Cover and chill until ready to use.
3. In a large bowl, toss chicken, apple, mango, celery and onion until well mixed.
4. Add reserved yogurt dressing and toss well.
5. Season with salt and pepper.
6. Serve and enjoy!

Strawberry Chicken Salad

Ingredients:

1/2 cup bottled poppy-seed dressing
1/4 cup minced green onions
3 tbsps. chopped fresh basil
1/2 tsp. freshly ground pepper
4 cups chopped cooked chicken
2 cups diced fresh strawberries
Salt to taste
1 cup chopped toasted pecans

Directions:

1. Stir together poppy-seed dressing, minced green onions, chopped fresh basil, and freshly ground pepper in a large bowl.
2. Fold in chicken and strawberries; add salt to taste.
3. Cover and chill 2 hours.
4. Stir in pecans just before serving.

Lemon-Basil Chicken Salad

Ingredients:

1 tbsp. chopped fresh basil
3 tbsps. olive oil
2 tsps. Dijon mustard 1 garlic clove, pressed
1/2 tsp. sugar
1/2 tsp. lemon zest
1/4 cup lemon juice
1/4 tsp. salt
4 cups chopped cooked chicken breasts
2 cups fresh baby spinach
1/3 cup diced sun-dried tomatoes

Directions:

1. Whisk together basil, olive oil, Dijon mustard, garlic, sugar, lemon zest, lemon juice, and salt.
2. Combine chicken, spinach, and sun-dried tomatoes in a large bowl.
3. Drizzle with basil mixture, tossing to coat.
4. Serve and enjoy!

Barley Chicken Salad with Goat Cheese, and Walnuts

Ingredients:

2/3 cup pearled barley
3 tbsps. extra-virgin olive oil
2 tbsps. sherry vinegar
1 tsp. Dijon mustard
3/4 tsp. kosher salt
1/4 tsp. freshly ground black pepper
2/3 cup seedless green and/or red grapes, halved
2 cups shredded boneless, skinless rotisserie chicken breast
1/3 cup chopped green onions
3 oz. goat cheese, crumbled
1/4 cup chopped walnuts, toasted
1 tbsp. fresh thyme leaves

Directions:

1. Cook barley according to package directions.
2. Rinse with cold water.
3. Combine oil and next 4 ingredients in a large bowl.
4. Add barley, grapes, chicken, and onions; toss well to combine.
5. Add cheese; toss gently to combine.
6. Sprinkle with walnuts and thyme.

Mixed Fruit Chicken Salad with Orange Raspberry Vinaigrette

Ingredients:

1/4 cup chopped pecans
4 cups chopped cooked chicken breasts
2 cups seedless red and green grapes, halved
2 celery ribs, chopped
1 (11-oz.) can mandarin oranges, drained
1 cup chopped fresh pineapple*
1/4 tsp. salt

Orange Raspberry Vinaigrette Ingredients:

1/2 cup orange marmalade
1/4 cup white balsamic-raspberry blush vinegar
1 med. jalapeno pepper, seeded and minced
2 tbsps. chopped fresh cilantro
2 tbsps. olive oil

Vinaigrette Directions:

1. Stir together all vinaigrette ingredients.
2. Set aside.

Directions:

1. Preheat oven to 350 degree F.
2. Bake pecans in a single layer in a shallow pan 6 to 7 minutes or until toasted and fragrant, stirring halfway through.
3. Toss together chicken and next 5 ingredients in a large bowl.
4. Add vinaigrette; toss to coat.
5. Sprinkle with pecans, and serve immediately.

Tzatziki Chicken Salad

Ingredients:

2/3 cup plain Greek yogurt
1/4 cup finely chopped red onion
1 tbsp. fresh lemon juice
2 tsps. chopped fresh dill
3/8 tsp. kosher salt
1/4 tsp. freshly ground black pepper 1 cucumber, seeded and shredded 1 garlic clove, minced
2 cups shredded skinless, boneless rotisserie chicken breast
3 oz. multigrain pita chips Mixed Greens Salad

Directions:

1. Combine first 8 ingredients in a medium bowl, stirring with a whisk.
2. Add chicken; toss to coat.
3. Serve with pita chips.

Chicken Salad with Olive Vinaigrette

Ingredients:

1 cup uncooked couscous
1/4 cup chopped pitted kalamata olives
2 tbsps. chopped fresh flat-leaf parsley
1 tbsp. chopped capers
2 tbsps. extra virgin olive oil
1 tbsp. fresh lemon juice
1/4 tsp. salt
1/4 tsp. freshly ground black pepper
1 garlic clove, minced
2 pkgs. (7-oz.) chicken breast in water

Directions:

1. Cook couscous according to package directions.
2. Drain and rinse with cold water.
3. Combine olives, parsley, capers, olive oil, lemon juice, salt, pepper and garlic in a large bowl, stirring with a whisk.
4. Add couscous to olive mixture; toss gently to coat.
5. Stir in chicken just before serving.

Chicken Salad with Nectarines in Mint Vinaigrette

Dressing Ingredients:

1 cup loosely packed fresh mint leaves
1/3 cup sugar
1/4 cup white wine vinegar
1 tbsp. fresh lemon juice
1/4 tsp. salt
1/4 tsp. freshly ground black pepper

Salad Ingredients:

2 cups chopped cooked chicken breast
1 cup chopped seeded cucumber
1/3 cup chopped pecans, toasted
2 tbsps. minced red onion
3 nectarines, chopped, peeled, and pitted
5 red leaf lettuce leaves

Dressing Directions:

1. Place mint and sugar in a food processor; process until finely chopped, scraping sides of bowl.
2. Add vinegar, juice, salt, and pepper, and process 30 seconds to combine.

Salad Directions:

1. Combine chicken, cucumber, pecans, onion, and nectarines in a medium bowl.
2. Drizzle dressing over salad; toss well to coat.
3. Place 1 lettuce leaf on each of 5 plates.
4. Top each serving with 3/4 cup salad.

Lemon Cashew Chicken Salad

Ingredients:

1 tsp. cumin seeds
1 tsp. coriander seeds
3 medium lemons
1 1/2 tbsps. butter
3 tbsps. minced fresh ginger
1 to 3 tbsp. finely chopped jalapeño chile
1/2 tsp. salt
1/3 cup mayonnaise
1/3 cup Greek yogurt
1/2 cup chopped fresh cilantro
1/2 cup chopped green onions
4 cups chicken, chopped
Chopped cashews

Directions:

1. In a medium frying pan over low heat, toast cumin and coriander seeds until fragrant, 3 to 5 minutes.
2. Transfer seeds to a spice grinder and process until finely ground.
3. Zest lemons and set aside zest.
4. Juice 1 lemon and set aside 3 tbsp. juice.
5. Melt butter in the frying pan over medium heat.
6. Add ginger, jalapeño, and salt.
7. Cook until jalapeño is soft, 3 to 5 minutes.
8. Remove from heat and set aside.

Lemon-Tarragon Chicken Salad

Ingredients:

1/2 cup chopped pecans
3/4 cup mayonnaise
1 tbsp. chopped fresh tarragon
1 tsp. grated lemon rind
1 tbsp. fresh lemon juice
1 tsp. salt
1/2 tsp. freshly ground pepper
3 cups chopped cooked chicken
2 celery stalks, finely chopped
1/2 small sweet onion, finely chopped
2 cups seedless red grapes, cut in half (optional)

Directions:

1. Arrange pecans in a single layer on a baking sheet.
2. Bake at 350 degrees F for 5 to 7 minutes or until lightly toasted.
3. Cool pecans on a wire rack 15 minutes or until completely cool.
4. Whisk together mayonnaise and next 5 ingredients in a large bowl.
5. Stir in pecans, chicken, celery, and onion just until blended.
6. Stir in grape halves, if desired.

Curried Chicken Salad with Apples and Raisins

Ingredients:

1/4 cup mayonnaise
1 tsp. curry powder
2 tsps. water
1 cup chicken, chopped
3/4 cup chopped Braeburn apple (about 1 small)
1/3 cup diced celery
3 tbsps. raisins
1/8 tsp. salt

Directions:

1. Combine mayonnaise, curry powder, and water in a medium bowl, stirring with a whisk until well blended.
2. Add the chicken, chopped apple, celery, raisins, and salt.
3. Stir mixture well to combine.
4. Cover and chill.

Melon Chicken Salad

Ingredients:

1/4 cup rice vinegar
2 tbsps. soy sauce
2 tbsps. chunky peanut butter
1 tbsp. honey
3/4 tsp. dark sesame oil
3 cups honeydew melon, cubed
3 cups cantaloupe, cubed
2 cups daikon radish, cubed
1 cup peeled English cucumber, cubed
3 tbsps. thinly sliced green onions
2 cups shredded cooked chicken breast
1/4 cup chopped fresh cilantro
2 tbsps. chopped walnuts, toasted

Directions:

1. Combine first 5 ingredients in a large bowl, stirring well with a whisk.
2. Add honeydew, cantaloupe, radish, cucumber and onions.
3. Toss well to coat.
4. Place 2 cups melon mixture on each of 4 plates; top each serving with 1/2 cup chicken.
5. Sprinkle 1 tbsp. cilantro over each serving.
6. Top each with 1 1/2 tsps. walnuts.

Chicken Salad With Grapes and Pecans

Ingredients:

1/2 cup mayonnaise
1/2 cup sour cream
1 tbsp. fresh lemon juice
1 tsp. salt
1/2 tsp. pepper
2 pounds skinned and boned chicken breasts, cooked and chopped
3 cups red and white seedless grapes, halved
1 cup chopped pecans, toasted

Directions:

1. Stir together 1/2 cup mayonnaise and next 4 ingredients in a large bowl.
2. Add chopped chicken and grapes, tossing gently to coat.
3. Cover and chill at least 1 hour.
4. Stir in pecans just before serving.

About the Author

Laura Sommers is **The Recipe Lady!**

She is the #1 Best Selling Author of over 80 recipe books.

She is a loving wife and mother who lives on a small farm in Baltimore County, Maryland and has a passion for all things domestic especially when it comes to saving money. She has a profitable eBay business and is a couponing addict. Follow her tips and tricks to learn how to make delicious meals on a budget, save money or to learn the latest life hack!

Visit her Amazon Author Page to see her latest books:

amazon.com/author/laurasommers

Visit the Recipe Lady's blog for even more great recipes and to learn which books are **FREE** for download each week:

http://the-recipe-lady.blogspot.com/

Subscribe to The Recipe Lady blog through Amazon and have recipes and updates sent directly to your Kindle:

The Recipe Lady Blog through Amazon

Laura Sommers is also an Extreme Couponer and Penny Hauler! If you would like to find out how to get things for **FREE** with coupons or how to get things for only a **PENNY**, then visit her couponing blog **Penny Items and Freebies**

http://penny-items-and-freebies.blogspot.com/

Other books by Laura Sommers

- **Recipes for Chicken Wings**
- **50 Super Awesome Salsa Recipes!**
- **Super Summer Barbecue and Pool Party Picnic Salad Recipes!**
- **50 Super Awesome Coleslaw and Potato Salad Recipes**
- **Homemade Salad Dressing Recipes from Scratch!**
- **50 Super Awesome Pasta Salad Recipes!**
- **50 Delicious Homemade Ice Cream Recipes**

May all of your meals be a banquet
with good friends and good food.

Made in the USA
Middletown, DE
06 February 2021

33264637R00038